TABLE OF CONTENT

I0467576

Preface

I came up with this book after I thought about the usefulness of the principles of mathematics taught in learning institutions and how their application is the finishing aspect. Yet the link between theory and application is not well emphasized in many fronts of education but is left to those that rise to universities to take on professions that are themselves scientific applications.

I thought that from me can come an input to benefit people worldwide. And here in this book is a build up to apply spearman's rank correlation to increase one's business profits. This book shows how by drawing the correlation between sales of commodities and overall profits, one can make correct or useful decisions to improve the profitability of a business.

There is prior knowledge needed to applying spearman's rank correlation. But no worries, in this very book one can be prepared through a whole chapter I have written and can qualify himself in taking on the lessons in the following chapters. Therefore you do not have to use further resources to search out for pre-requisite knowledge so as to following through the correlation application; the book itself shall qualify you.

By using this book you will also gain knowledge on adding and subtracting fractions, substituting in a formula, making the subject, solving simultaneous equations using the substitution, elimination and matrix methods.

Data related to the problem is examined so as to formulate mathematical relationship between variables in the problem.

CHAPTER 1

PREAMBLE

This course aims at enriching students of statistics, students of business, students of mathematics, business men and women.

The data and situations presented in this book are hypothetical.
Therefore hypothesis has been applied so as to pave way for empirical modeling and to enable the reader to practically perceive and apply the benefits of this book.

Here is a situation; you own a business whose profits are inconsistent and low and you are in a state of decision making so as to redeem the business and boost it. But you know not where to start from.

Let us say you are selling shoes and belts, ideally an equal amount of quantity of shoes is sold within the time and with the same pattern. So the overall profits of the business can easily be viewed as largely coming from the shoes since they would be of higher price. However you would find difficulty in determining which commodity positively influences the sales of the other.

Now what if one day after another the number of belts and shoes sold keep alternating, quantities of one being sold on a day being greater than another and the other getting greater on the following day. Leading to one commodity staying in stock longer than another and the profits being inconsistent, leading to delayed recovery of capital and making of profits.
However if there be knowledge on which commodity determines the sales of another, then strategies can be made to stabilize and boost the business. What if belts are sold because those who come to buy the shoes

desire to buy a matching belt after they have bought a particular pair of shoes?

Also what if particular shoes are not bought simply because a customer did not find a matching belt, may be to match color or pattern or design.

If you know such a thing, then you can make strategic stocking and marketing of your business so as to draw customers and to sell the shoes equally as quickly as the belts.

Therefore this course provides a step by step guide to knowledge of correlation and its application in business so as to make better the profits earned.

By applying the knowledge of correlation to a business enterprise, one can discover the strength of dependence of one commodity to another in terms of quantity sold. Also how each commodity impacts on the overall profits made in the business.

After making such findings, a business owner can confidently alter quantities stocked per commodity, advertisements made or products produced so as to increase and make stable the profits being realized.

Whereas I have used a two commodity situation this can also be applied to a business of multiple commodities, by pairing commodities of interest in that business and finding their contributing strength to the business.

This application of the rank correlation can reduce on the risks encountered in operating a business.

OBJECTIVES

By the end of this course, the learner should be able to;

> ➤ Add and subtract fractions.
> ➤ Make the subject.
> ➤ Substitute in a formula.

➢ Solve simultaneous equations.

➢ Multiply matrices and find inverse of a matrix.

✓ Calculate the Rank correlation coefficient using the spearman's formula.

✓ Comment on the rank correlation coefficient value.

✓ State from the rank correlation value and comment, how one commodity sold depends on another commodity sold in the same business.

✓ State from the obtained rank correlation value and

comment, how each commodity sold influences the amount of profits made in the entire business.

✓ Make correct and informed decision on which commodity to improve, adjust or eliminate through quality control, marketing and advertisement and quantity control.

✓ Appreciate the use empirical modeling in solving world problems.

<u>BENEFITS</u>

1. Acquisition of knowledge on application of spearman's rank correlation in computation.
2. Acquisition of business profit analysis skills.

3. Acquisition of the knowledge of where and how to increase business profits by applying spearman's rank correlation.

BENEFICIARIES

1. Students of statistics
2. Students of business studies
3. Students of mathematics
4. Business people.

EXERCISE 2

1. What knowledge and skills would you have acquired by the end of this course?
2. What measures can you take to improve the profitability of a business as regards the commodities sold and profits made?

CHAPTER 2

PRE-REQUISITE

MATERIALS REQUIRED

MATERIAL	USE
1. A CALCULATOR	COMPUTING
2. WORK BOOK	KEEP PERSONAL NOTES
3. A RULER	DRAWING LINES
4. A PENCIL	TABLE DRAWING
5. A PEN	WRITING NOTES

PRIOR KNOWLEDGE

1. Addition, subtraction, multiplication, and division of fractional and non-fractional numbers.
2. Ability to read and write English.
3. Ability to use a mathematical calculator.
4. Ability to round off decimal numbers.

5. Ability to square numbers
6. Ability to obtain the average of ungrouped data.
7. Ability to substitute into a formula
8. Ability to list given integers in terms of greater or less
9. Ability to Make the subject in a formula
10. Knowledge on matrix order, multiplication and matrix inverse.

REVIEW OF PRE-RQUISITE TOPICS

2.1 FRACTIONS

Examples
Work out;

1. $\dfrac{5}{7} + \dfrac{3}{14}$

Solution

By first obtaining the lowest common multiple (LCM) of 7 and 14

Diving thru by 7	7	14
Diving thru by 2	1	2
	1	1

Therefore LCM is 7 x 2 = 14

$$\frac{5}{7} + \frac{3}{14} = \frac{5 \times 2 + 3 \times 1}{14} = \frac{10+3}{14} = \frac{13}{14}$$

2. $\dfrac{-4}{5} + \dfrac{1}{6}$

Solution

By first obtaining the LCM of 5 and 6

Dividing thru by 2	5	6
Dividing thru by 3	5	3
Dividing thru by 5	5	1
	1	1

Therefore LCM is 2 x 3 x 5 = 30

$3. \ 1 - \dfrac{42}{11}$

Solution

Changing 1 into a fraction;

$\dfrac{1}{1} - \dfrac{42}{11}$, LCM of 1 and 11 is 11

Therefore

$$\dfrac{1}{1} - \dfrac{42}{11} = \dfrac{(11x1) - (42x1)}{11}$$

$$= \dfrac{11-42}{11} = \dfrac{-31}{11} = -2\dfrac{9}{11}$$

$4. \ \dfrac{4}{15} \div \dfrac{2}{3}$

Solution

The division sign is changed into a multiplication sign and the fraction immediately after the division sign to the right is reciprocated.

Thus, $\dfrac{4}{15} \div \dfrac{2}{3} = \dfrac{4}{15} \ x \ \dfrac{3}{2} = \dfrac{4 \ x \ 3}{15 \ x \ 2} = \dfrac{12}{30}$

Reducing both the numerator and denominator by 6,

$$\frac{12}{30} = \frac{2}{5}$$

EXERCISE 2.1

Work out;

1. $\frac{3}{16} + \frac{5}{8}$ 2. $\frac{-3}{5} - \frac{9}{10}$ 3. $\frac{2}{3} - \frac{2}{5}$

4. $\frac{3}{10} + \frac{-5}{8}$ 5. $\frac{-3}{4} - \frac{5}{12}$ 6. $\frac{1}{7} - \frac{-3}{4}$

7. $\frac{5}{6} + \frac{3}{4}$ 8. $\frac{1}{3} - \frac{3}{8}$ 9. $1 - \frac{2}{9}$

10. $1 - \frac{-95}{28}$

2.2   SUBSTITUTING IN FORMULA

Examples

1. Find the value of P in the formula P = 2q-3r when q = 3 and
r = -5.

Solution

P = 2x3 – 3x-5

= 6 - - 15

= 6 + 15

= 21

1.Find the value of W in the formula W = xy + z when x = 1.2 ,
 y = 3.2 and z = 2.0.

Solution

W = 1.2x3.2 + 2.0

   = 3.84 + 2.0

   = 5.84

1. Find the value of A in the formula $A = x^2 - 2y^2$, when x =2 and y=3

Solution

$A = 2^2 - 2x3^2$

  = 4 − 2 x 9

  = 4 - 18

  = - 14

Exercise 2.2

1. Find the values of B in each of the
   following if x = -2, y = 3 and
z = -5.
a) B = 2x + 3y   b) B = 4x − 3y
c) B = 5(x − 2y)   d) B = 3(-3x + z)

e) B = x^2-y^2 f) B = z^2- y^2

g) B = 3yz − zx   h) B = y(y + z)^2

i) B = 4(x + y)^2

2. If a = 2.6, b = -3.2 and c = 1.4, find y
   when
a) y = a − b + c   b) y = abc
c) y = -6a − 4b   d) y = ac − 5

e) y = $\dfrac{a+4b}{c}$ f) y = 4a − 5b
g) y = 3ac − 3b^2

h) y = b(2b − 3c) i) y = c^2 + b^2

3.If y = mx + c , find y when;

a)m = 1.5 , x = -4 ,c = 5

b) m = -4, x = 1 ,c = -3

c) m = -7, x = 0, c = 10

d) m = 0, x = 8, c = -2

e) m = -3, x = -2, c =4

f) m = 2, x = -4, c = -6

g) m = 1, x = -6, c =-2

h) m = -1, x = 5, c = 3

2.3   MAKING THE SUBJECT

Make x the subject in the following formulae.

1. $ax + c = p$ 2. $a(x + q) = k$

3. $X^2 + y = m$ 4. $\dfrac{2c}{3x} - 7 = b$

Solutions

1. Subtracting c from both sides of the equation

$ax + c - c = p - c$

$ax \quad = p - c$

dividing both sides of the equation by a

$$\frac{ax}{a} = \frac{p - c}{a}$$

Therefore

$$x = \frac{p - c}{a}$$

1. Dividing through by a

$$\frac{a(x + q)}{a} = \frac{k}{a}$$

$$x + q = \frac{k}{a}$$

Subtracting q from both sides of the equations.

$$x + q - q = \frac{k}{a} - q$$

$$x = \frac{k}{a} - q$$

1. Subtracting y on both sides.

$$x^2 + y - y = m - y$$

$$x^2 = m - y$$

Taking the square root on both sides

$$\sqrt{x^2} = \sqrt{m - y}$$

$$x = \sqrt{m - y}$$

3. Adding 7 on both sides

$$\frac{2c}{3x} - 7 + 7 = b + 7$$

$$\frac{2c}{3x} = b + 7$$

Multiplying through by 3x

$$3x \times \frac{2c}{3x} = (b + 7) \times 3x$$

$$2c = 3x(b + 7)$$

Dividing both sides by 3(b + 7)

$$\frac{2c}{3(b+7)} = \frac{3x(b+7)}{3(b+7)}$$

$$\frac{2c}{3(b+7)} = x$$

Therefore,

$$x = \frac{2c}{3(b+7)}$$

Exercise 2.3

1. Make y the subject in each of the following formulae

a) V=y(2-3at)

b) G=k(y-ct)

c) $M = \frac{b-a}{y-a}$

d) $a = \frac{y+at}{s}$

e) $\frac{a}{b} = \frac{c}{y}$

f) yh = d – n

2. Make w the subject in each of the following formulae

a) $(w - r)^2 + c = d^2$

b) $v = \sqrt{\frac{w-c}{b}}$

c) $d = \sqrt{wb} - 5$

d) $b^2 = c^2 + w^2$

e) $\frac{1}{f} = \frac{1}{w} + \frac{1}{v}$

f) $v = a\left(\frac{1}{b} - \frac{1}{w}\right)$

1.4 MATRICES

Determinant of a matrix

For a given 2 x2 matrix M,the determinant is the difference between the product of the major diagonal and the product of the minor diagonal. Denoted as det M.

Example

Give the determinant of the following matrices.

$$1.\begin{pmatrix} 2 & -7 \\ 1 & 4 \end{pmatrix} \qquad 2.\begin{pmatrix} 4 & -3 \\ 2 & 5 \end{pmatrix}$$

Solution

1. (2x4) – (-7x1) = 8 - -7 = 8 + 7 = 15
2. (4x5) – (-3x2) = 20 - -6 = 20 + 6 = 26

Ad joint of a matrix

To find the ad joint of a matrix, the position of numbers in the major diagonal are interchanged while the sign of each number in the minor diagonal takes the opposite sign.

Example

Find the ad joint matrix of the following matrices.

1. $\begin{pmatrix} 5 & -2 \\ 6 & 7 \end{pmatrix}$ 2. $\begin{pmatrix} -5 & 3 \\ 1 & 9 \end{pmatrix}$

Solution

1. $\begin{pmatrix} 7 & 2 \\ -6 & 5 \end{pmatrix}$ 2. $\begin{pmatrix} 9 & -3 \\ -1 & -5 \end{pmatrix}$

Inverse of a matrix

This is the product of the reciprocal of the determinant and the ad joint matrix.

Let A be a 2 x 2 matrix, then

Inverse A $(A^{-1}) = \dfrac{1}{\det A}$ x **Ad joint A**

Example

Find the inverse of the following matrix.

1. $\begin{pmatrix} 6 & -2 \\ -3 & 9 \end{pmatrix}$

Solution

Let **M** = $\begin{pmatrix} 6 & -2 \\ -3 & 9 \end{pmatrix}$ then det M

= (6x9) – (-2x-3)

= 54 – 6

=48

And ad joint **M** = $\begin{pmatrix} 9 & 2 \\ 3 & 6 \end{pmatrix}$

Therefore,

M^{-1} = $\dfrac{1}{48}$ x $\begin{pmatrix} 9 & 2 \\ 3 & 6 \end{pmatrix}$

$$= \begin{pmatrix} \dfrac{9}{48} & \dfrac{2}{48} \\ \dfrac{3}{48} & \dfrac{6}{48} \end{pmatrix}$$

$$= \begin{pmatrix} \dfrac{3}{16} & \dfrac{1}{24} \\ \dfrac{1}{16} & \dfrac{1}{8} \end{pmatrix}$$

Exercise 2.4

Find the inverse of the following matrices.

1. $\begin{pmatrix} 4 & 6 \\ -2 & 1 \end{pmatrix}$
2. $\begin{pmatrix} 2 & 1 \\ 6 & 7 \end{pmatrix}$

3. $\begin{pmatrix} -4 & -1 \\ -4 & 2 \end{pmatrix}$
4. $\begin{pmatrix} 2 & 0 \\ 1 & 4 \end{pmatrix}$

5. $\begin{pmatrix} 0 & 2 \\ -1 & 5 \end{pmatrix}$
6. $\begin{pmatrix} 10 & 7 \\ \dfrac{3}{2} & 13 \end{pmatrix}$

7. $\begin{pmatrix} 6 & 2 \\ 1 & 9 \end{pmatrix}$
8. $\begin{pmatrix} 1 & 1 \\ 2 & 3 \end{pmatrix}$

9. $\begin{pmatrix} 2 & 3 \\ 4 & -3 \end{pmatrix}$
10. $\begin{pmatrix} 15 & 3 \\ 4 & \dfrac{1}{2} \end{pmatrix}$

2.5   SIMULTANEOUS EQUATIONS

Example 1

Solve the simultaneous equations below by substitution method;

$a - b = 3$ ------------ equation 1

$a + 2b = 9$ ------------equation 2

Solution

Making a the subject in equation 1

By adding b on both sides of the equal sign

$a - b + b = 3 + b$

$a = 3 + b$ --------------- equation 3

a being the subject in equation 3.

Substituting for a in equation 2.

$3 + b + 2b = 9$

$3 + 3b = 9$

$3 + 3b = 9$

subtracting 3 on both sides of the equal sign;

$3 - 3 + 3b = 9 - 3$

$3b = 6$

Dividing through by 3;

$$\frac{3b}{3} = \frac{6}{3}$$

b = 2

Substituting for b in a = b + 3

$$a = 2 + 3$$

$$a = 5$$

Example 2

Solve by elimination method the simultaneous equations

5x − 2y = 13 ------------equation 1

X + y = 4 ------------- equation 2

<u>Solution</u>

Inspecting the coefficients of x in equation 1 and equation 2, their magnitudes are different.

Also the coefficients of y in equation 1 and equation2, their magnitudes are different. Therefore by multiplying 2 through equation 2,

X + y = 4 becomes

2x + 2y = 8 -----------------equation 3

Comparing equation 1 with equation 3

$5x - 2y = 13$

$2x + 2y = 8$

Now that the coefficients of y are of the same magnitude, by adding the two equations y is eliminated.

$5x - 2y = 13$

$+\ \ 2x + 2y = 8$

$\overline{\ \ \ 7x\ + 0\ = 21}$

$7x = 21$

Dividing through by 7

$$\frac{7x}{7} = \frac{21}{7}$$

$X = 3$

Making y the subject in equation 2

$y = 4 - x$

Substituting for x,

$y = 4 - 2$

$y = 2$

Example 3

Use matrix method to solve the simultaneous equations below.

$2x + y = 4$ ------------ equation 1

$y - x = 1$ ------------ equation 2

Solution

Rearranging the left hand side of equation 2 so that x is aligned as the first unknown in the first term.

$2x + y = 4$

$-x + y = 1$

It follows that

$$\begin{pmatrix} 2 & 1 \\ -1 & 1 \end{pmatrix}\begin{bmatrix} x \\ y \end{bmatrix} = \begin{bmatrix} 4 \\ 1 \end{bmatrix}$$

Where 2 and -1 in the first column of the leading matrix are coefficients of x in equation 1 and equation 2 respectively. And 1 and 1 in the second column of the leading matrix are coefficients of y in equation 1 and equation 2 respectively.

The determinate of the leading matrix being,

(2x1) – (1x-1) = 2 - -1 = 2+1 = 3

Ad joint of leading matrix being, $\begin{pmatrix} 1 & -1 \\ 1 & 2 \end{pmatrix}$

Then the inverse is

$\frac{1}{3}\begin{pmatrix} 1 & -1 \\ 1 & 2 \end{pmatrix}$, multiplying this inverse on the left hand side of every side of the equation;

$$\frac{1}{3}\begin{pmatrix} 1 & -1 \\ 1 & 2 \end{pmatrix}\begin{pmatrix} 2 & 1 \\ -1 & 1 \end{pmatrix}\begin{pmatrix} x \\ y \end{pmatrix}$$

$$= \frac{1}{3}\begin{pmatrix} 1 & -1 \\ 1 & 2 \end{pmatrix}\begin{pmatrix} 4 \\ 1 \end{pmatrix}$$

The product of the inverse of a matrix and that matrix gives an identity matrix (this is a matrix whose major diagonal has 1 and 1 and the minor diagonal is made up of zeros only

$$\begin{pmatrix} 1 & 0 \\ 0 & 1 \end{pmatrix}\begin{pmatrix} x \\ y \end{pmatrix} = \frac{1}{3}\begin{pmatrix} (1x4) + (-1x1) \\ (1x4) + (2 \times 1) \end{pmatrix}$$

On the right hand side the principle of matrix multiplication was followed. Row by column.

$$\begin{pmatrix} 1 & 0 \\ 0 & 1 \end{pmatrix}\begin{pmatrix} x \\ y \end{pmatrix} = \frac{1}{3}\begin{pmatrix} 4 + -1 \\ 4 + 2 \end{pmatrix} = \frac{1}{3}\begin{pmatrix} 3 \\ 6 \end{pmatrix}$$

Therefore,

$$\begin{pmatrix} x \\ y \end{pmatrix} = \begin{pmatrix} \frac{1}{3} \times 3 \\ \frac{1}{3} \times 6 \end{pmatrix} = \begin{pmatrix} 1 \\ 2 \end{pmatrix}$$

Thus x = 1 and y = 2

Exercise 2.5

1. Use elimination method to solve the following pairs of simultaneous equations.

a) x = y + 3

   x + 2y = 9

b) c = d + 1

   2c + d = 14

c) 4a - b = 10

   a + 3b = 9

d) 3a + b = 8

     b = a − 12

e) x + y = 5

     x − y = 1

f) 3x + 2y = 6

     2x − 3y = 17

2. Use substitution method to solve the following pairs of simultaneous equations.

a) y = 3x

   2x − y = -6

d) x + 2y = 6

    x = 3y − 9

b) c = 7 − 2d

e) 2x + y = 12

$3c - 2d = 9$ $3x - y = 13$

c) $4m - n = 6$ f) $5a + 2b = -8$

$3m + 2n = -1$ $a - 3b = -5$

3. Use matrix method to solve the following pairs of simultaneous equations.

a) $b = 2a - 3$ d) $c = 3d - 1$

   $a + 3b = 5$ $5c - 7d = 19$

b) $x = 1 - y$ e) $5m - 2n = 13$

   $3 = y + 2x$ $m + n = 4$

c) $5x + y = 12$ f) $2m + 3n = -1$

   $3x + 2y = 3$ $m + 4n = 2$

CHAPTER 3
CORRELATION

This is the measure of the degree of association between two or more variables. Correlation can be positive or negative.

POSITIVE CORRELATION

Correlation is positive when the increase of one variable results in the increase of another variable

Examples

- Suppose you visited a doctor for advice on health and fitness and he advises you to jog regularly and visit the gym on a weekly basis. After a month you find out that you have lost weight. Then you can say that there is positive correlation between regular exercising and weight loss.
- If every time you wake up in the night and do extra reading, your exam grades

get better; then you can say that there is positive correlation between extra reading and better grades.

NEGATIVE CORRELATION

Correlation is negative when the increase of one variable results in the decrease of another variable or the decrease of one variable results in the increase of another variable.

Examples

- ❖ Suppose every time you eat a meal when you are stressed your appetite is low. And the more stressed you are the more you lose your appetite. Then you can say that there is a negative correlation between stress and appetite.
- ❖ Suppose every time you have little money in your pocket you are happier and when you have lots of money in your pocket you are less happy. Then

you can say there is a negative correlation between money in your pocket and happiness.

EXERCISE 3

Briefly explain the following, giving two examples in each case.

    a) Positive correlation

    b) Negative correlation

CHAPTER 4

SPEARMAN'S RANK CORRELATION COEFFICIENT FORMULA

$$\rho = 1 - \frac{6\sum d^2}{n(n^2 - 1)}$$

$\sum$ = **Means Summation**

ρ = **Stands for the spearman's Rank Correlation Coefficient.**

n = **Number of pairs of variables**

d = **Deviation. This is the difference of ranks.**

Let v_1 = variable 1, v_2 = variable 2, R_1 = rank of v_1 and R_2 = rank of v_2 then;

$$d = R_1 - R_2 \text{ and thus}$$
$$d^2 = (R_1 - R_2)^2$$

EXERCISE 4

Name and state any other formula that can be used to calculate the Rank Correlation coefficient.

CHAPTER 5

THE SQUARE OF DEVIATION

Consider the table below having two variables P and Q.

Table 1.0

P	Q
12	11
32	24
14	65
25	23
16	27
09	18

The first step is to generate Ranks for each entry. For a given variable you assign 1 to the highest up to 6 (in this case) in descending order respectively.

Table 1.1

P	Q	R_P	R_Q
12	11	5	6
32	24	1	3
14	65	4	1
25	23	2	4
16	27	3	2
07	18	6	5

Where R_P and R_Q are ranks of P and Q respectively.

Now after obtaining the ranks, you obtain the deviation (d) which is the difference between the ranks per row.

Table 1.2

	Q	R_P	R_Q	d
12	11	5	6	-1
32	24	1	3	-2
14	65	4	1	3
25	23	2	4	-2
16	27	3	2	1
07	18	6	5	1

Remember d = (R_P – R_Q)

And the now you can square d.

Table 1.3

P	Q	R_P	R_Q	d	d^2
12	11	5	6	-1	1
32	24	1	3	-2	4
14	65	4	1	3	9
25	23	2	4	-2	4
16	27	3	2	1	1
07	18	6	5	1	1

EXERCISE 5

Calculate the deviation (d) of the variables in table 2 below and hence the square of deviation (d^2).

Table 2

X	8	12	6	4	13	1	7	5	10	11	16	3
Y	4	9	8	1	10	2	7	15	6	12	13	3

CHAPTER 6
DECIMAL OR REPEATED RANKS

Consider table 3 below; using the knowledge so far acquired and fixing the ranks of X.

Table 3

X	Y	R_X
29*	24	2
34	44	1
29*	24	3
11	24	5
13	35	4

You can notice that 29 appears twice. Now it is **not** correct, neither is it fair for a number just the same to have different ranks. So you take the average of the two ranks and assign the result to each one of the 29s.

$$\text{Average} = \frac{2+3}{2} = \frac{5}{2} = 2.5$$

So in table 4.0, you have the correct writing of the ranks.

✓ Table 4.0

X	Y	R$_X$
29	24	2.5
34	44	1
29	24	2.5
11	24	5
13	35	4

EXERCISE 6

1. Copy and complete the table below.

Table 4.1

X	Y	R$_X$	R$_Y$	d	d^2
29	24	2.5			
34	44	1			
29	24	2.5			
11	24	5			
13	35	4			

2. Rank the variables p and q in table 5 below and find the deviation.

Table 5

P	31	46	50	31	15	34	11	31	63	45

CHAPTER 7
CALCULATING THE RANK CORRELATION COEFFICIENT

Now consider in a business where two commodities are sold simultaneously in the same business are sold simultaneously in the same business.

If below is the table of the number of items sold for two commodities and the profits within 8 weeks on a weekly basis.

Table 6

Week	1	2	3	4	5	6	7	8
Commodity1 X 100	2	1.5	1.8	0.6	1.9	2.1	1.6	0.75
Commodity2 X100	3	0.8	1.1	2	0.7	0.48	0.9	1.2
Profits($)X100	90	38.5	43.5	49	42.5	41.1	42	35.25

The questions I would ask are; how does commodity 1 depend on commodity 2 in terms of sales? Are they dependent or not? To what extent is this dependence?

You will have to calculate the rank correlation so as to get answers to those questions. Consider table 7.

Let 1 and 2 represent quantity of commodity 1 and commodity 2 sold respectively.

Table 7

1	2	R_1	R_2	d	d^2
200	300	2	1	1	1
150	80	6	6	0	0
180	110	4	4	0	0
60	200	8	2	6	36
190	70	3	7	-4	16
210	48	1	8	-7	49
160	90	5	5	0	0
75	120	7	3	4	16
					$\Sigma d^2=118$

Key

1 =sales of commodity 1

d^2 = square of deviation

2= sales of commodity 2

$\sum d^2$ = total sum of d^2

R_1 = Rank of 1

R_2 = Rank of 2

d = deviation ($R_1 - R_2$)

It is now time to apply the spearman's rank correlation coefficient formula to calculate coefficient.

$$\rho = 1 - \frac{6\sum d^2}{n(n^2 - 1)}$$

$$= 1 - \frac{6 \times 118}{8(64-1)}$$

$$= 1 - \frac{708}{504}$$

$$= \frac{504 - 708}{504}$$

$$= \frac{-204}{504}$$

$$= -0.4048 \text{ (4dp) cal}$$

This number has a meaning. This shall be looked into in the next chapter.

EXERCISE 7

Calculate the Rank correlation coefficient of data in table 2 and table 5 from chapter 5 and 6 respectively.

CHAPTER 8

TABLE OF COMMENTS OF POSITIVE AND NEGATIVE RANK COEFFICEINTS

POSITIVE VALUES

This part contains two tables showing the comment made when the Rank correlation is positive or negative.

Table 8

RANK	COMMENT
0 – 0.19	Positive chance correlation
0.2 – 0.39	Positive weak/low correlation
0.4 – 0.59	Positive moderate correlation
0.6 – 0.79	Positive strong/high correlation
0.8 – 0.999	Positive very strong/high correlation

NEGATIVE VALUES

Table 9

RANK	COMMENT
-0 to -0.19	Negative chance correlation
-0.2 to -0.39	Negative weak/low correlation
-0.4 to -0.59	Negative moderate correlation
-0.6 to -0.79	Negative strong/high correlation
-0.8 to -0.999	Negative very strong/high correlation

Therefore the comment for -0.4048 is;

There is a negative moderate correlation between the quantity of commodity 1 and quantity of commodity 2 sold.

EXERCISE 8

1. Provide a comment for each of the following rank correlation coefficient values.

a) 0.424

b) 0.79

c) 0.112

d) -0.621

e) -0.2

f) -0.816

g) 0.278

h) -0.0092

2. In table 9.1, 9.2 and 9.3 below, find the correlation between x and y using spearman's rank correlation coefficient formula and comment on each value obtained.

Table 9.1

X	7	22	15	12	25	8	18	5	10
y	10	36	18	20	42	12	28	2	12

Table 9.2

X	18	27	10	12	15	22	30	5	8	20	24
y	3.2	3.8	17	12.8	8	6.8	5	17	15.2	5	2.6

Table 9.3

X	25	7	15	25	22	18	5	9	12	13	6
y	62	13	27	57	53	46	7	19	18	21	5

CHAPTER 9

Interpretation

This means that as the number of items of commodity 1 sold go up, those of commodity 2 go down or as number of items of commodity 2 go up, those of commodity 1 go down.

The number of items sold affect each other negatively but moderately.

EXERCISE 9

For every comment that you made in activity 8 under lecture 8, give an interpretation.

CHAPTER 10

Profits and commodity 1

The question is; which commodity influences profit making positively more than the other.

Table 10.0

Commodity 1	Profits(P)	R_1	R_P	d	d^2
200	9000	2	1	1	1
150	3850	6	7	-1	1
180	4350	4	3	1	1
60	4900	8	2	6	36
190	4250	3	4	-1	1
210	4110	1	6	-5	25
160	4200	5	5	0	0
75	3525	7	8	-1	1
					Σd^2=66

Calculating spearman's rank correlation coefficient;

$$\rho = 1 - \frac{6 \times 66}{8(8^2 - 1)}$$

$$= 1 - \frac{396}{504}$$

$$= \frac{504 - 396}{504}$$

$$= \frac{108}{504}$$

$$= 0.2143 \text{ (4dp) cal}$$

<u>Comment</u>: There is a weak positive correlation between number of items of commodity 1 sold and profits made.

EXERCISE 10

If below are amounts of commodity A and B sold and profits made per day in 10 days. Calculate the spearman's rank correlation coefficient between quantities of A sold and profits made, comment on your result and give an interpretation.

Table 10.1

A	23	31	60	20	19	16	22	51	38	16
B	40	36	71	18	24	32	24	54	33	15
Profits ($)	86	98	191	58	62	64	68	156	109	47

CHAPTER 11

Profits and commodity 2

Table 11

Commodity 2	profits	R_2	R_p	d	d^2
300	9000	1	1	0	0
80	3850	6	7	-1	1
110	4350	4	3	1	1
200	4900	2	2	0	0
70	4250	7	4	3	9
48	4110	8	6	2	4
90	4200	5	5	0	0
120	3525	3	8	-5	25
					$\sum d^2 = 40$

Computing spearman's rank correlation coefficient

$$\rho = 1 - \frac{6 \times 40}{8(8^2 - 1)}$$

$$= 1 - \frac{240}{504}$$

$$= \frac{504-240}{504}$$

$$= \frac{264}{504}$$

$$= 0.5238 \text{ (4dp) cal}$$

Comment

There is a positive moderate correlation between number of items of commodity 2 sold and profits made.

CONCLUSION

This means selling commodity 2 leads to more profits compared to selling of commodity 1.

Therefore possibly the business decision would be to devise ways of increasing the number of items of commodity 2 sold more than of commodity 1, this is what would increase the profits of the business.

EXERCISE 11

1. Using table 10.1 in Exercise 10, calculate the spearman's rank correlation coefficient between quantities of B sold and profits made, then comment and give interpretation.

2. A business owner records sales for commodities A,B and C as shown in the table 12 below. By calculating the spearman's rank correlation coefficient, what advice can you give to the business owner in order to have increased and stable profits?

Table 12

Day	1	2	3	4	5	6	7
A	40	60	56	60	63	70	53
B	12	10	16	21	40	18	50
C	42	58	51	59	61	57	54
Profits ($)	86	108	111	131	172.5	128	180.5

CHAPTER 12

ANALYSIS

RESULT ANALYSIS

Let me compute the total sales per commodity.

Table 13

COMMODITY	1	2	PROFIT
	200	300	9000
	150	80	3850
	180	110	4350
	60	200	4900
	190	70	4250
	210	48	4110
	160	90	4200
	75	120	3525
TOTAL SALES	1225	1018	

You notice that the total number of items of commodity 2 sold are lower than those of commodity 1, yet commodity 2 determined the profitability of the business more than commodity 1.

<u>Findings</u>: This means that though the business owner did not disclose the profit per item sold for each commodity; commodity 2 per item brings in more profits than commodity 1, provided the prices per item are not altered.

<u>Investigations:</u>

Suppose you become curious to find the profit per item per commodity made.

Then;

You assign $\$x$ profit for each item of commodity 1 sold and you assign $\$y$ profit for each item of commodity 2.

Then choosing any two pairs; for instance let me pick row 2 and row 3 from table 13.Two simultaneous equations are formed;

$200x + 300y = 9000$ equation 1
$150x + 80y = 3850$ equation 2

Simplifying equation 1 and 2, we obtain
$2x + 3y = 9$ (after eliminating 2 ending zeros) equation 3
$15x + 8y = 385$ (after eliminating 1 ending zero) equation 4

Now solving by substitution equation 3 and 4;

Making x the subject in equation 3,

$$x = \frac{90 - 3y}{2}$$

And substituting in equation 4, it follows;

$$15\left(\frac{90-3y}{2}\right) + 8y = 385$$

$$15(90-3y) + 8y\text{x2} = 385\text{x2}$$

$$1350 - 45y + 16y = 770$$

$$-45y + 16y = 770 - 1350$$

$-29y = -580$ **Dividing through by -29 we obtain**

$$\frac{-29y}{-29} = \frac{-580}{-29}$$

$$y = 20$$

Therefore $x = \dfrac{90-3(20)}{2}$

$$= \frac{90-60}{2}$$

$$= \frac{30}{2}$$

$$x = 15$$

Therefore each item of commodity 1 fetched a profit of $15 and each item of commodity 2 fetched a profit of $20.

Alternatively,

Using matrix method of solving,

Consider table 13 row 2 and row 3,

$$\begin{pmatrix} 200 & 300 \\ 150 & 80 \end{pmatrix} \begin{pmatrix} x \\ y \end{pmatrix} = \begin{pmatrix} 9000 \\ 3850 \end{pmatrix}$$

Let M = $\begin{pmatrix} 200 & 300 \\ 150 & 80 \end{pmatrix}$

Ad joint M = $\begin{pmatrix} 80 & -300 \\ -150 & 200 \end{pmatrix}$

Determinant M = (200x 80) – (300x150)

$$= 16,000 - 45,000$$

$$= -29,000$$

Therefore inverse M =

$$\frac{-1}{29,000} \begin{pmatrix} 80 & -300 \\ -150 & 200 \end{pmatrix}$$

$$\frac{-1}{29,000}\begin{pmatrix} 80 & -300 \\ -150 & 200 \end{pmatrix}\begin{pmatrix} 200 & 300 \\ 150 & 80 \end{pmatrix}\begin{bmatrix} x \\ y \end{bmatrix}$$

$$= \frac{-1}{29,000}\begin{pmatrix} 80 & -300 \\ -150 & 200 \end{pmatrix}\begin{pmatrix} 9000 \\ 3850 \end{pmatrix}$$

Thus;

$$\begin{pmatrix} 1 & 0 \\ 0 & 1 \end{pmatrix}\begin{bmatrix} x \\ y \end{bmatrix} = \begin{pmatrix} 15 \\ 20 \end{pmatrix}$$

$$x = 15 \quad and \quad y = 20$$

Therefore each item of commodity 1 brings $15 profit and each item of commodity 2 brings $20 profit.